MW01248290

MOUNTAIN
LESSONS

Life Lessons Learned
While Hunting Elk in the
Mountains of Montana

BY JERRY ROSS

Ultimate Goal Publications
Jasonville, Indiana
www.stayinthecastle.com

MOUNTAIN LESSONS

"I was happy in the midst of dangers and inconveniences."
Daniel Boone

MOUNTAIN LESSONS

Table of Contents

Dedicated to
Doug, Derek, and Ron
— good men to share a campfire with.

INTRODUCTION

I'm not an elk hunter. Southern Indiana does not provide Hoosier outdoorsmen with that opportunity. It has, however, provided me a lifetime of enjoyment through fishing and hunting. My passion is bow hunting Whitetail deer, and, like most honest hunters, I have some trophies on the wall as well as stories about some big bucks that were almost on the wall.

It has always been a dream of mine to one day go out West on an elk hunt. I was able to see that desire become a reality in the fall of 2015. An opportunity arose for me to hunt public ground in the Montana mountains, and I was blessed to harvest a young 5x5 bull on the first day of my hunt.

I spent the balance of the five-day hunt assisting the other men in our group as we climbed and scouted, waited, as well as stalked these majestic animals. And always, there were plenty of things to learn along the way. Mountain lessons were learned — some serious, some humorous, but all important to this Indiana flat-lander. These are man-size lessons, sadly lost to a generation of young men who view adventure, challenge, and hardship as things to be avoided instead of sought out.

But in every generation there are still men who feel born out of time. To these men, I share this book, hoping it will help you climb whatever mountain calls you.

Jerry Ross

Chapter 1

DO IT WHILE YOU CAN

"The mountains are calling, and I must go." John Muir

Everyone of us will go to our graves with some unfulfilled dreams. Especially if you truly are a dreamer. There is a lot to do, a lot to see in this world. There is also real life. And life's parameters will never allow any of us to get to it all.

But there are some endeavors that you should just decide to find a way to do, especially if you are getting a bit long in the tooth. An elk hunt was a thirty year itch that I had never been able to scratch, and as I talked to my good wife about it, I told her, "If I'm going to do this, I'd better do it while I can."

Most dreams seem unreachable because we do not sit down and outline what is needed to achieve that dream. I often refer to the Bible patriarch, Jacob, who dreamed a dream, and in this dream was a ladder that ascended from *where* he dreamed to *what* he dreamed. This ladder had steps, and each step was designed to take him a bit closer to the realization of his dream. Before you give up on whatever you dream of doing, at least take the time to sit down and draw out the ladder.

My elk hunt was going to require both time and money. As for the time, I needed to be able to get away for eleven days — two days to travel there, the Lord's day in church, five days to hunt, and three days to get back (two days of travel and another Lord's day in church).

The cost of the trip, like any trip, boiled down to four

elements — travel costs, lodging costs, food costs, and the hunting costs (license, equipment, etc.)

Many of these costs can be minimized. Travel costs can be shared if you go with one or two friends. Same with motel costs. Much of your travel food can be brought from home.

As far as hunting equipment, several men offered to lend us the things that we needed for the hunt. I am always careful borrowing things, but because of the generosity of others, I did not have to buy everything that was needed.

An out of state hunting license is expensive, and something that you have to save up to purchase. Or, you might have to sell some things to afford it. Again, you have to ask yourself, how badly do you want to go?

Run the numbers: travel, lodging, food, hunting costs. To achieve anything in life, you must first count the cost.

Then, get the blessing of two people in your life: your wife, and God. If you are going to ask your wife to be OK with you going on a trip like this, then you'd better understand that you owe her! A nice vacation for her next year would be in order. If you are blessed with a wife that is supportive of an occasional hunting trip, you are a blessed man.

As to getting God's permission, I would always encourage you to make sure that whatever you plan is within the will of God. If it is, things will work out for you to go. If it isn't, stay home!

Doug Cassel is a good friend and fellow pastor. We had talked of going elk hunting for years, and decided that talking wasn't doing, so we decided to pursue the dream and go.

At the end of my life, I will not regret the dreams I pursued and achieved, but very likely will regret the dreams I simply dreamed. So, if possible, do it while you can!

Chapter 2

FIND A MOUNTAIN MAN

*"That some achieve great success is proof to all
that others can achieve it as well." Abraham Lincoln*

Whatever mountain in life you aspire to climb, there is someone who has already successfully scaled it. You can try it on your own, and you may succeed, but you increase your chances dramatically if you will find a mentor. In our case, we needed a proven, elk-hunting, mountain man!

Our first option was Eric, a friend of mine who lives here in Indiana. He has traveled out West numerous times and the elk mounts adorning his home are witness to the fact that he knows what he is doing. So in the Spring of 2015, Doug and I approached him seeking advice, when to our delight he offered to travel out with us. We were excited to say the least! It is always better to go with someone who has "been there, done that." Eric had hunted elk in Colorado, so that became our chosen destination.

Later that summer, Eric contacted me to tell me that circumstances had changed. The plant where he worked was on outage, and he was being put on seven days of work a week for the next several months. His advice, "plan on me not being able to go with you." Although we were disappointed, we trusted the Lord and moved ahead with our preparations.

Doug and I began to look for someone with elk hunting experience to accompany us on the hunt. Common sense dictated that our chances of success (as well as survival!) would greatly increase. We priced guided hunts, but for us, they were simply unaffordable. Then, in a very surprising way, God opened up a totally different opportunity.

In early September, I had scheduled an evangelist to come in and preach our Fall revival. I picked him up at the airport, and on our drive from there to the hotel, the conversation turned to hunting. I shared with him my dilemma, not knowing that he had, for a time, lived out West.

"The preacher, who discipled my wife and I, now pastors in Montana, and has for the last 27 years. He is an avid elk hunter, and might agree to take the two of you hunting with him for a week. His name is Ron. I'll give him a call."

A week after that conversation, everything worked out. We were heading to the Montana mountains to hunt elk! During my first telephone conversation with this Montana preacher, I learned that he had hunted elk for 27 years and had harvested 23 elk in that time period. That is an unheard of success rate! It was an honor to accept his kind invitation.

When Montana became our destination, I called another friend who lives there. Derek grew up in Montana, and is now an assistant pastor there. He worked it out to go, so instead of one Montana mountain man, we had two. Our hunting foursome consisted of: Doug and myself, Ron, and Derek.

The greatest way to succeed in life is to find someone who is a success in the area in which you desire to succeed. Then listen to him. I told Ron that Doug and I were outdoorsmen but not elk hunters, and that we would be pleased to learn everything we could from him. For a week, we listened, asked questions and followed his advice. What he taught me contributed greatly to my success.

Want to climb a mountain? Find a mountain man!

Chapter 3

GOOD COMPANY MAKES ANY TRIP BETTER

"It is far better to be alone, than to be in bad company."
George Washington

Growing up, I subscribed to a variety of outdoor magazines. It was always a good day when the mailman left a *Field & Stream, Outdoor Life,* or *Guns & Ammo* magazine in the mailbox. Looking back, what I learned from those hunting stories was as much about integrity as it was about skills and tactics.

I remember one article in particular that made a big impression upon my young mind. It was written by a man who made his living as a hunting guide. Every year, he would take a variety of clients on guided hunts. This would require him to spend a week in the company of these men. As you might suspect, not every trip was enjoyable. He told some horror stories about men whose personalities, ethics, and general behavior made the week close to unbearable. He also said that these men, thankfully, were the minority. His best and kindest words were reserved for the men who were honorable, helpful, and humble — good hunters, but better men. He concluded his article, "Strive to be the kind of man with whom good men would be pleased to share a campfire."

My friend Eric, (who was unable to go with us on the hunt) told us a story of a man who accompanied him on a hunt to Colorado years ago. He was a friend of a friend, and Eric agreed to take him along. Four of them in all climbed into a truck and headed for Colorado. Almost from the get-go, he knew bringing this man was a mistake. He had an abrasive personality. He tried to figure out how not to pay his part of the fuel expense and complained about every decision made. When they arrived in Colorado, he shirked his share of the camp work. Later that week, Eric killed a bull elk, which infuriated this guy. He accused Eric of choosing the best place to hunt and assigning him to a place where there would be no elk. He refused to help pack meat off the mountain, instead going off to continue his own hunt. By the time the week was over, it was all Eric could do not to physically lay hands on the guy.

Don't ever be THAT guy!

There are a few character traits that real men will not long tolerate in their companions.

Selfishness. A man who is focused only on himself is not a man you want to share a camp with.

Complaining. No one can long tolerate a whiner.

Boasting. The Good Book says, "Let another man praise thee, and not thine own mouth; a stranger, and not thine own lips." That's pretty good advice.

Laziness. Always pull your own weight.

Vulgarity. Anyone who thinks that swearing or blaspheming God's name makes him a man is sadly mistaken.

Cheating. Pay your own way. Be fair in your dealings.

Thievery. Not many things worse than a thief.

Angry. There is no place in a hunting camp for a hothead. The Bible warns us, "An angry man stirreth up strife."

I enjoyed a great week of hunting for many reasons. But high on the list is this: Doug, Derek, and Ron were good men to share a campfire with.

And I hope they felt the same.

Chapter 4

TEMPER YOUR EXPECTATIONS

*"A hunt based only on trophies taken falls far short
of what the ultimate goal should be."* Fred Bear

In most parts of Montana, you have less than a 20% chance to harvest a bull elk. That means you might have to go five years in a row to take one bull elk. Or, if five of you hunt together, you can expect one hunter to succeed. Everyone wants to take an elk, but as you plan your trip, you have to temper your expectations.

Eric asked me a great question when I first brought up the subject of an elk hunt. "Jerry, what do you want out of this trip?"

I pondered the question and gave an honest answer. "I want to go and camp out in the mountains, enjoy God's creation and clear my mind. Oh, and if I kill an elk in the process, that would be a bonus."

His response was telling. "If you go with that attitude, you are going to have a great time." He went on to explain that too many guys are so focused on the goal of harvesting a bull elk that they fail to enjoy the most important parts of the experience. If they fail to take a bull, then they count the entire trip a failure.

Most of our disappointments in life are due to the fact that we entered into a relationship or an endeavor with unrealistic expectations. No person or no experience can possibly live up to what we insist he/she/it to be. What I am saying is this: if you are going to go home mad if you don't kill an elk, then don't go! Because chances are four out of five of you are going home mad.

Eric asked a great question. "What do you really want out of this trip?" Let me ask you a greater question. "What do you really want out of life?"

Most people, who live their lives discouraged, disappointed or angry do so because their expectations are unrealistic. They expect a level of perfection from people that no one can live up to. Your wife, your husband, your children, your friends, your family — they are all human. If they are sincere, and are doing the best they can, then let that be good enough.

Same is true with life's experiences. Learn to temper your expectations. I know it sounds corny, but the journey is as important as the destination — so enjoy the journey. We have created a society that is so goal oriented and success driven that it has robbed us of the enjoyment of everyday pleasures. Some of the greatest hunts I have ever enjoyed did not include pulling a trigger or releasing an arrow. For those who pay attention, there is always something new to see and always something new to learn. Nature is one of the greatest classrooms on the planet.

Set goals and strive to achieve them. But also, learn to be realistic in life. Control what you can control, and put the rest in God's hands. Decide ahead of time that you are going to have a great time whatever the outcome of the hunt.

Or whatever the outcome of life.

Chapter 5

GET IN SHAPE

"With self-discipline, most anything is possible." Theodore Roosevelt

In my first conversation with Ron, he asked me a pretty straight-forward question.

"What kind of shape are you two in?"

Here were two Baptist preachers from Indiana asking to go hunting with him for a week, neither of whom he had ever met. Sadly, like most Americans, many preachers are overweight and out of shape. Can't say I blamed him for asking.

Doug and I had been preparing with the expectation that we would be hiking five to seven miles a day in Colorado's Rocky Mountains, so we both were in reasonably good shape.

This Montana elk hunter was pretty hard-core. He is 70 years of age and in remarkably good health. He also is strong as a bull. I watched him bring down a 90 lb. pack of elk meat off the mountain. He is Montana tough!

Hiking five to eight miles a day was our average at altitudes ranging from 6000-7800 feet above sea level. Our hunt was scheduled for the first week of November, well past the rut, so the elk were not going to come to us, we had to go to them.

Hunting in the Montana mountains in November is pretty basic. We climb the back side of the mountain before dark each morning, so that we can be at the top trying to catch the elk coming up after spending the night feeding. In the evening, we climb up the mountain ravines within shooting distance of the top trying to catch them coming down to feed. During the day, we stalk-hunt the high timbers. This involves a lot of climbing so you have to be in reasonably good shape.

Being in good physical, mental and spiritual shape makes everything in life much easier. It increases your chances of success in all endeavors. Even if you think you are in good shape, there is no test like the mountains out West.

For me, getting in shape required losing a bit of weight and building up physical endurance.

I did not have to lose much weight. I have weighed myself regularly for the past 20 years. I stay in the window between 190 lbs. and 200 lbs., which fits my 6'2" frame. I did trim down to 185 before I left on our hunting trip. Weight management is not about gimmick diets or infomercial, magic-weight-loss pills. Ideal weight is achieved and maintained by managing your intake, and increasing your output. Eat less and exercise more and you will lose weight.

I did need to build up physical endurance. I walked and jogged off and on throughout the summer, but honestly should have been more consistent. That thin Montana mountain air and the steep mountain terrain whipped me pretty bad the first two days. I hiked about 7 miles the first day we hunted, helped pack my elk down the mountain the next morning, then hunted again that second evening. I was wrung out the first two evenings. I did seem to do better the last three days, as my body and lungs adjusted to the challenge.

Whether you are planning a mountain hunt or not, let me encourage you to begin to work at getting into reasonably good shape. Limit your intake (healthier foods and reasonable portions) and increase your output (evening walks and basic exercises). Before you start, go see your doctor. He will be the one to best guide you through the process.

Chapter 6

BROADEN YOUR PERSPECTIVE

*"It suddenly struck me that that tiny pea, pretty and blue, was the
Earth. I put up my thumb and shut one eye, and my thumb blotted
out the planet Earth. I didn't feel like a giant. I felt very, very small."*
Neil Armstrong

Our hunting accommodations were unusual, but amazing. The Montana preacher who allowed us to hunt with him also was kind enough to offer to share his hunting "cabin" with us. This cabin was a 1980 Chevrolet bus that was gutted and refitted with two sets of bunk beds, a propane stove, propane heaters, and shelves for storing food and gear. He drove this bus an hour past the last vestige of civilization, parked it near a creek, and we had instant camp.

Three nights of our hunt, it dropped into single-digit temperatures at night. Yet the propane heaters kept the bus comfortably in the mid 50s. That may not sound very warm, but remember, we are talking perspective. Come in from hiking through the snow with temperatures in the teens for an entire morning and 55 degrees seems balmy.

The Apostle Paul wrote, "I know how to be abased, and I know how to abound." The people who appreciate life the most are those who have tasted the widest range of human experience. The greater the hunger, the more the appreciation of food. The coldest man most appreciates the fire. Wealth can only truly be appreciated by someone who has experienced poverty. We all need to be "abased" in order to appreciate the "abound."

From time to time, all of us should leave our comfort zone so that, when we return, we can truly appreciate the comfort. I have more than once taken teenagers on a church mission's trip to a third-world country. Once a teenager spends a week living amongst true poverty, he is ashamed to come home and complain about what he doesn't have. What changed? Just one thing — his perspective.

I love the western mountains. If you have never visited the Rocky Mountains, make a point to do so. It truly is a spiritual experience. Hiking through the mountains has a way of helping you see yourself differently. We think we are so big, but the mountains dwarf us. Our life is a bleep on the radar compared to the age of these mountains. We are born, we live, we die, yet the mountains endure.

It is amazing just how little humans really need to survive. I had warm clothes, good food, and a comfortable place to sleep each night. Fry some bacon, eggs and red potatoes in an iron skillet over a fire, and it tastes better than anything produced by the finest five-star restaurant. Stare up at the stars in Big Sky country, and you know without a doubt that Someone greater than you created them. Watch the sun rise over an 8000 foot snow-capped peak and it puts a lump in your throat. Hear the elk bugle the day awake and the wolves howl it to sleep, and you just want to get down on your knees and thank God you were allowed to be there.

My friend Eric said it best. He told me a week in the mountains "cleanses your soul."

Yep. And it also puts a lot of things back into perspective.

Chapter 7

IT ONLY SEEMS TO BE EASIER GOING DOWN THAN UP

"The heights by great men reached and kept were not attained by sudden flight, but they, while their companions slept, were toiling upward in the night." Henry Wadsworth Longfellow

During our five-day hunt, I did a lot of climbing up and down. Climbing up a mountain requires more energy than going down, but in every other way, climbing up was easier than climbing down. That's right, *up* was easier.

Our bodies were not designed to descend. The only time my knees hurt was when I was climbing down. Your leg and feet muscles as well as your skeleton are not designed for steep descent. It was as if our Creator purposefully designed humans to climb — to go upward, not downward.

It is much more dangerous climbing down than up. When you ascend the mountain, you naturally lean your body into the climb, and your center of gravity helps balance you. If you fall, you fall into the slope where you can easily catch yourself with your hands. Plus, no one has ever fallen forward and rolled up a mountain!

Climbing down, you have to lean unnaturally backward to keep your balance. Your feet shift down into the toes of your boots, and your leg muscles and knee cartilage are under constant strain. I never fell going up the mountain, but did fall several times descending. Those falls are the ones that are most likely to cause serious injury.

Many a man has looked at the paths of life and been tempted to take what appears to be the easiest direction. After all, it may seem logical that going down is easier than going up. A lower life may at first seem more appealing than an upward life, but for those who choose to descend, they soon find that it takes a taxing and terrible toll.

The song writer wrote...

I'm pressing on the upward way,
New heights I'm gaining every day,
Still praying as I'm onward bound,
Lord, plant my feet on higher ground.

A man who chooses low morals, shallow character and carnal standards will soon find his life in a downward spiral. It always seems easier to do wrong than to do right, especially when the vast majority of humanity seems to be heading into the low swamps of depravity. But I would again remind you, going down will, in the long run, take a greater toll on you than climbing upward.

God waits on the mountain. Those who want the sweetest fellowship with Him must climb. Up at the top is rare air! If you make the effort, you will often have to do it alone. The good news — it's never crowded at the top. But the few men and women who are up there are worth getting to know.

Like I said, it may not at first seem logical. And yes, it might take more energy to climb up than down, and it might take a little longer getting to the top than descending to the bottom.

But who ever stood at the base of a mountain and whispered, "What a view!"

Chapter 8

GET RID OF
UNNECESSARY WEIGHT

*"We can easily manage if we will only take, each day,
the burden appointed to it."* John Newton

Every elk hunter carries a backpack. It is used both to carry your gear into the mountains, and to pack your meat out of the mountains. Every hunter has to decide what he wants to carry in his back pack.

Cabela's, Gander Mountain, Scheels, and other sporting goods stores have entire aisles filled with things you can talk yourself into needing! Especially if you are a rookie elk hunter like I was. Snake bite kits, flare guns, bear mace, emergency tents, extra flashlights and batteries fill the shelves along side waterproof matches, air sirens, rain gear, emergency rations, and foot blister medicine. Then there are the knives (yes — plural — I thought I needed at least four), bone saws, extra rifle ammo, rope, tarps, game bags, an extra pistol, and 50 rounds of pistol ammo.

On top of that I needed water, extra water, snacks, extra snacks, as well as extra clothing — socks, sweatshirts, hats, and extra gloves. Hand warmers, foot warmers, and body warmers were added to my walkie-talkie, my GPS, and my cell phone. That first morning all this was packed, and I was ready for any and every situation the mountain could throw at me.

The first day, we hiked around 7 miles up and down the mountains. I dressed in layers, and as the sun came up and the temperatures rose, layers of clothes came off and were strapped to my backpack. As the day progressed, to my annoyance, the back pack seemed to miraculously increase in weight! By mid-afternoon, I felt like I was carrying a boulder on my back. All these "necessities" were making my day miserable.

When we finished the first day I was exhausted. Time to make some tough decisions! I unzipped my backpack emptied it out, then asked myself, "What do I really NEED, and what is just extra weight?'

Every man carries a backpack. This is only right, since every man should carry his own burden. But each of us must decide what we put in that backpack. There are necessities, then there are some things that are just dead weight.

I see a lot of people who are overburdened. They live their lives physically, mentally and spiritually exhausted. Many are carrying things that the Bible warns us not to hold on to. Bitterness weighs a man down. Jealousy, envy, and an unforgiving spirit will, over time, become millstones. I've watched grief drag men and women to their graves. Some things in life you have to just let go. They just are not important enough to carry, and they are sapping you of the enjoyment of the journey.

From time to time, every one of us needs to unzip our back packs, take everything out, and consider what we really NEED to be carrying. If it is needful, then man up and shoulder it. But if it is just dead weight, leave it lay.

After all — a flare gun? Really?

Chapter 9

DRINK WHETHER YOU ARE THIRSTY OR NOT

"The Bible has never failed to give me light and strength."
Robert E. Lee

When it comes to the weather, the biggest difference between the Midwestern states and the Western states is the humidity. The air out West is dryer. Because of this, their heat is a "dry heat" and their cold is a "dry cold." The effect of this is that it does not feel as hot or as cold as it does in Indiana. This affects the body in a strange way. You do not seem as thirsty in the West as you do the Midwest. Because of this, it is easy to spend the day hiking and not feel the need to hydrate.

Here is the rule: drink whether you are thirsty or not.

Doug told me that when he was in the military, good soldiers constantly reminded their buddies to hydrate. Everyone in the platoon kept everyone else accountable.

My backpack contained a water bladder with a tube running from the backpack to my front shoulder. I could drink often just by turning my head and sucking on the tube. This kept my hands free and movement to a minimum.

The Montana preacher also encouraged us to take snacks with us on the hunt and nibble on something often. This keeps your digestive system active, or as he put it, "keeps your furnace running." So, into the backpack went peanut butter sandwiches and high protein trail mix, along with an extra bottle of Gatorade.

The problem is, most of the time, you don't feel much like eating and you don't feel thirsty. But even if you don't, you follow the rule. Drink and eat whether or not you feel thirsty or hungry.

Proper intake is key to maintaining your stamina. Dehydration can make you nauseous and light headed. Rob your body long of food and you soon lose strength and warmth. Inadequate intake puts you and those with you at great risk.

Reading the Bible is the same way. It is our spiritual food and drink. The Word of God is compared to milk, bread, and meat. We also read of the "water of the Word." Most people only read the Bible when the feel they need it. If they are discouraged, or going through a valley, then they will break out the Bible and read. But if all seems to be going well in life, it sits gathering dust for weeks at a time.

As a Christian, you should pass a rule concerning your spiritual intake: read the Bible daily whether you think you need it or not. Insufficient intake affects your spiritual health.

The way most Bibles are printed, reading five pages of the Bible a day will get you through the Bible in a year. Every day I start the day by reading the Bible. If I am on page 205, I read to page 210. Then read five more pages the next day. This takes about 10 minutes a morning. Think of that! Every one of us could read through the entire Bible every year if we would just discipline ourselves to read for 10 minutes a day.

The person who is the most convinced that they do not need to read the Bible is the person who needs it the most. Try it for 30 days. See if it does not begin to make a difference in your life. Create accountability with a friend. Check on each other, and make sure proper intake is maintained.

Chapter 10

TAKE ONE STEP
AND LOOK FIVE TIMES

"And what I say unto you I say unto all, Watch." Jesus Christ

Doug and I spent most of our camp time just listening to Ron, the old Montana preacher. We asked a lot of questions about hunting, his church and ministry, and life in general. One evening, Doug asked him a great question.

"What's the best piece of hunting advice you were ever given?"

Ron leaned back and shared a story. "Years ago there was an old Indian hunter who was somewhat of a legend in these parts. People tried to get him to tell them the secret to his unparalleled hunting success. Finally, one day when pressed, he shared one observation."

"When a white man hunts, he takes five steps and looks once. When an Indian hunts, he takes one step and looks five times."

I mused on this piece of advice the next morning as I hunted. I don't know if this will happen or not, but I had to smile at this thought: what if God replayed every hunt I was ever on, and the number of times I walked right past game that I never saw. How many times has a deer passed within bow range of my stand and I just failed to see him. Most of us have "busted" out deer on our way to our tree stand, or, once in our stand, glanced down to suddenly see a deer right beneath us that seemed to have magically appeared out of nowhere.

One of the reasons that I encourage young men to get into hunting is because it will help develop their character. Hunting requires patience and hones your observation skills. Often, while Whitetail hunting, a deer was seen because I simply noticed a flick of an ear, or the movement of a tail. Most things in the woods grow vertically. Learning to look for horizontal lines in dense cover will often allow you to see a deer before it sees you.

Rare is the man who has mastered the gift of observation. Most of us are in too much of a hurry. We walk right past opportunities that a more careful, thinking man would notice. Every great invention was created by someone who first saw a need. Ever see something new and innovative for sale in a store and say to yourself, "Why didn't I think of that?" Someone not only observed a problem, but took the time to figure out how to fix it.

Careful observation skills are also important because every man carries the responsibility of protecting himself and his loved ones. Learn to look around. A man should always be scanning and assessing potential danger. He should also be the first to act — to steer himself or his family out of harms way — or the first to react if avoiding harm is not an option.

Observation skills also allow you to see opportunities to help people. There are needs everywhere, but sadly, most of us hurry by without a second look. Jesus was masterful at noticing people who others overlooked, and taking the time to stop and be a blessing.

Everyone looks, but few see. Learn to be one of the few.

Chapter 11

THIS CRAZY, UNBELIEVABLE THING CALLED LIFE

"We are all here for just a spell, so get all the good laughs you can."
Will Rogers

Life is full of crazy, humorous moments. This trip was no exception.

Ron, our Montana host, is a godly man. The entire focus of his life is serving the Lord — well, that and elk hunting. Modern day culture holds no interest to him.

He told us about listening to a sermon where a preacher mentioned Hannah Montana. Having lived for almost three decades in Montana, he was shocked he had never heard of this town! He spent an evening searching an atlas before his son told him about the young pop star.

————————————

After our first evening of hunting, Doug got back to the bus before us. He radioed Ron and said he would start supper. Doug then radioed back to ask Ron if he had any cooking oil.

"No, you will have to use bacon grease."

Doug rummaged around the cooler, then radioed back, "Where's the bacon grease?"

Brief silence. Then over the radio came Ron's answer.

"In the bacon."

I couldn't stop laughing, but instead of being embarrassed, Doug was excited. "Every time we want to fry something, we will have to fry bacon first. That means bacon at every meal!"

For most guys, that is pretty much heaven.

———————————

On our Tuesday evening hunt, we scaled the mountain and set up to glass for elk. At some point, I took out my cell phone to take a few pictures of the mountains. No signal that far out, so all it was good for was a camera. I laid it on a rock beside me, hunted till dark, then gathered my gear to hike down the mountain. When I got to camp, I discovered I had left my phone on the mountain. No way I was hiking back up in the dark, so I decided I'd get it the next day.

In the middle of the night, nature called, so I got up and put on my boots to go out. When I opened the bus door, I discovered that it had snowed about 4 inches! My first thought was my cell phone. I figured it was ruined.

After hunting the next morning, Doug and I hiked back up to where I left it. (He was thrilled to take an extra climb up the mountain because of my forgetfulness!) I had hunted the south side of the mountain, and the sun had heated the rock my phone laid on, melting the snow. I said a quick prayer, turned it on and it worked fine. Thank the Lord and Otter Box!

———————————

The bus "hunting cabin" we were staying in was amazing. The propane heaters kept it a very comfortable 50 degrees at night, however the single-digit night-time temperatures outside the metal bus produced some amazing results. We woke up to find my hunting vest frozen to the windshield, and our hunting boots frozen to the floor of the bus.

How awesome is that?

———————————

Ron has pastored in Montana for 27 years. Like many

Western pastors, he is bi-vocational. That means he is willing to work jobs on the side to provide for his family while still fulfilling the duties of a full-time pastor. Gotta tip your hat to that level of dedication.

He decided to start his own hauling business. He secured a semi truck and trailer, and began to move small, prebuilt cabins into the mountains. Most of these were being hauled to remote locations reached only by traversing winding mountain backroads. Not a job for the faint of heart.

He told us that on one such trip, he encountered a hairpin turn that his rig simply could not make. On his right was the steep mountain, and on his left a sheer drop off. The man he was hauling the cabin for had a track hoe, so the two of them came up with a plan. The owner of the track hoe backed up to the rear of the semi-trailer, hooked on and swung the trailer out over the drop off so that Ron could make the turn!

You just can't make this stuff up.

————————-

Before hunting elk out West, do some basic homework.

Ron told us of two East Coast men who decided to try elk hunting. Neither were experienced outdoorsmen, but somehow lucked their way into killing two cows on their first day of the hunt. They were excited and managed to quarter the animals and load them into their truck.

All went well until they showed up at a DNR office to check in their kills. That is when they discovered the difference between a cow elk and a cow moose.

Yep, they both had shot moose instead of elk. Conservation officers have no sense of humor about such things.

————————-

We decided to take Doug's truck on our trip out West.

He owns a 2007 Chevrolet Avalanche that I refer to as his "yuppie truck." Our camp was nine miles off the last county road, and the one lane, rocky tracks we drove for those nine miles were rugged. It took us over an hour to go that distance. After it snowed, we couldn't get in or out without tire chains.

At the end of one of our morning hunts, we agreed to meet at his truck. It was a long hike off the mountain, and I happened to get there first. I radioed the other hunters.

"You are not going to believe what I found."

Derek answers, "What?"

"Somebody parked a yuppie truck on the mountain."

Derek, "Must be some city slicker."

"I'll check the glove box for registration papers."

Silence.

"This truck is registered to someone named Hannah Montana."

Doug then got on the radio to inform us we were all walking back to town.

———————————

On the drive back from Montana to Indiana, we plotted a course that would take us by the maximum number of Cabela's. Yep, we checked out seven "bargain caves" in two days travel time. Been there, done that, got the t-shirts.

———————————

Some of the greatest memories of any hunting trip are the crazy, humorous things that happen along the way. The Good Book teaches us, "A merry heart doeth good like a medicine." Learning to see and enjoy the lighter side of life improves your mental outlook and your physical health.

So learn the great secrets to happiness — laugh often, never buy a yuppie truck, and eat lots of bacon.

Chapter 12

BE WILLING TO PAY THE PRICE

"There has never been a man in our history who led a life of ease whose name is worth remembering." Theodore Roosevelt

At 4:30 each morning, the alarm would go off in our bus cabin. The old Montana hunter would get up and start lighting the propane lanterns.

"Let's go, men, you can't kill elk in your bunks."

As I mentioned before, this man had taken 23 elk in 27 years. He would kill his 24th by the end of the week. Remember, this is in a state with a 20% hunting success rate for elk. Doug asked him what made him a better hunter than most.

"I wouldn't say that I am a better hunter," he told us. "I probably just work harder at it than most."

If you are going to succeed at anything in life, you have to be willing to pay the price.

Ron announced to us that he would only be able to hunt with us the first half of the day on Thursday. That afternoon he would head back to his house to pick up his wife, son and daughter-in-law and go Whitetail hunting. They had obtained a total of 20 tags for a deer management hunt at one of the local ranches. That evening, the family accounted for 14 deer harvested. Ron then field dressed all 14, loaded them up, hung them in his garage, and was back elk hunting on Friday morning. As a family, they try to put 1000 pounds of meat in the freezer each Fall.

Friday morning, instead of coming all the way to camp,

he parked on the other side of the mountain and hiked up before first light. For the next 6 hours he hiked and hunted, stalking and shadowing elk, but was unable to get off a shot. He radioed me just after lunch and asked if I would drive and pick him up down the road from camp. I drove about a mile and found him. He was smiling and had a story for me.

"A couple of guys in a pick-up truck just stopped and chatted with me. They were driving the roads looking for elk. They complained that they had only cut one set of tracks in the fresh snow and wondered why there were not more elk."

"I told them I had cut 14 fresh sets of tracks that morning. They asked me. 'Where?' I just pointed to the top of the mountain. They said, 'But what would you do if you killed one way up there? I mean, how would you get the meat down?'"

"I told them that we had already packed one off the mountain earlier this week. They just shook their heads and drove off."

He called people like this "truck hunters." Their hunting strategy boiled down to driving the back roads in a warm truck, sipping beer while listening to Willie Nelson, all the time hoping to spot an elk wandering near the road. Not a well thought out plan if you wish to consistently fill your tag.

Ron made a 428 yard shot on a cow elk the next evening. The cow fell 600 yards from the top of the mountain and, yes, we packed the meat down. The Montana preacher worked hard for that elk, and God blessed his efforts.

The level of satisfaction you experience from any endeavor will always be in direct proportion to the difficulty of that endeavor. Done right, mountain hunting is hard work, but the pay off is worth the effort: memories of a lifetime, and if you are fortunate, fresh back straps!

Chapter 13

THE IMPORTANCE OF FOOTPRINTS

"I have never been lost, but I will admit to being confused
for several weeks." Daniel Boone

We woke up on Wednesday morning to four inches of fresh snow. Snow is always good when elk hunting. It makes the elk easier to spot when you are glassing, as well as provides us a chance to track the elk.

We were up early and drove around to the back side of the mountain to climb up before shooting light. I had shot my bull elk on Monday evening, and was just hoping to fill a wolf tag. That morning, I was hunting with Derek. Our plan was to climb up the mountain together, then split up to hunt separately. Derek was raised in Montana, and much more familiar with the mountains than I am. He also is a lot younger and in better shape than I am. I was slowing him down, so I encouraged him to go ahead at his own faster pace.

He asked me, "Do you know where you are going?" I smiled and told him, "I'll just follow your footprints till I get to the top."

For the next thirty minutes, I paced myself and finished the 1500 foot climb up the rocky slope. I had learned that for this flat-lander, slow and steady wins the race. I never worried about getting lost, because leading the way was a set of footprints. All I had to do was put my foot in his footprints and I was assured to get to the top.

I had a clip light that I attached to the bill of my cap. It illuminated the footprints with enough light to show me my next step. Simple enough.

The Christian life isn't as hard as we sometimes make it out to be. Jesus said to follow in His steps. He also provided for us a light to illuminate His steps.

"Thy word is a lamp unto my feet, and a light unto my path." (Psalms 119:105) Read the Bible and let it guide you.

On Thursday morning of our hunt, I was following the Montana pastor up the mountain. It was still dark when we arrived at the top, and we were in the tall timbers. There had been another fresh snow fall during the night. He told me that we needed to split up. The plan was to meet back at this same spot in a couple of hours. I did not have my bearings yet, and was a bit worried about getting turned around in the dark.

"What if I get lost and can't find my way back here?" He looked at me for a moment, then down at my feet.

"If you get lost, follow your footprints backwards until you get to a place where you weren't lost."

Oh.

And they say there are no dumb questions.

When I got back to Indiana, I told the story of my "dumb question" to our church teenagers and repeated Ron's simple, common sense advice. After they stopped laughing, I told them this:

"I want you all to remember that advice. If you ever lose your way — I mean, for some reason you get off the right path in life, don't be too proud to admit it. Pushing on in the wrong direction just makes things worse. Instead, turn around, and follow your footprints back to where you weren't lost."

I pray none of them ever gets lost. But if one does, I hope that advice might someday get him or her back home.

Chapter 14

SLOW AND STEADY
WINS THE RACE

"It is not the mountain we conquer, but ourselves."
Edmund Hillary, first man to scale Mt. Everest

Mountain air is thin. You run out of breath quickly when you are climbing a mountain. My mountain friends again gave me good advice.

"Stop when you get winded. Slow your breathing for about a minute, then continue your climb. Don't push yourself to the point of exhaustion. Slow and steady wins the race."

A man named Aesop wrote a tale about a turtle that beat a jack rabbit in a race. Slow and steady almost always finishes ahead of fast but fickle. If you live to be seventy years of age, God will have given you 25,570 days give or take a few. The best plan is to consistently accomplish something every day. Make some progress. Chip away at your goals. It is amazing what consistent daily effort adds up to in a lifetime.

The Holy Bible instructs us, "...let us run with patience the race that is set before us." Life requires a marathon mentality. It is not a sprint, so our run must be managed with patience. One of the most important skills in life is the ability to pace yourself.

The older you get in life, the smarter you have to work. Old man time is undefeated, so you have to learn to do what you can, as you can. But don't quit. You quit, you die.

In my dad's latter years, he once told me, "Jerry, I'm

only good for about a half a day." This, from a man who worked more in his life than most men do in two lives.

My answer to him? "Dad, then do half a day."

Everyone has a different pace in life. For those of you, who are young and full of youthful strength and energy, don't waste it. Use it to help those in your family and your community who need a helping hand. Get off the couch, turn off the video games, and do something useful.

Derek was the fourth man in our group. Doug told me that Derek is built like an Army Ranger — medium framed and wiry but strong and built to go forever. When we were packing the meat off the mountain, he would head down faster than any of the rest of us, but he did so for a reason. Once he got to camp, he emptied his pack and immediately headed back up to pack down any extra meat. Once, he came back just to help one of us get our pack off the mountain. If God has blessed you with youthful strength and health, use it to be a blessing to those around you.

Live life with a good, steady pace. Learn to be consistent, keep moving forward, and stop and rest when you need to. If you do this every day, over your lifetime, you will accomplish more than you can imagine.

From what I've heard, the turtle still has a winning record against that rabbit.

Chapter 15

BRING GOOD GLASS

"Lord, I pray thee, open his eyes, that he might see."
Elisha the prophet

I phoned Ron several times as I was preparing for the elk hunt. His advice was always valuable. One of our conversations was on the subject of hunting equipment.

"Bring good glass," was his advice.

What he was telling me was don't go cheap on your optics. A good pair of binoculars or good spotting scope, a good range finder, and a good scope for your rifle are essential.

Every one of us is for saving money where we can. But one of the lessons you learn early is this: you get what you pay for. You do not have to buy the most expensive item available, but more times than not, if you buy the cheapest, you will wish you would have added a few more dollars and bought a better quality item.

The reason quality optics are important on a trip out West is because the human eye has its limitations. You can only clearly see so far.

His advice proved invaluable. We had hunted hard the first morning, and met back at camp mid-afternoon to decide where to hunt in the evening. All four of us decided to hunt Derksen Mountain. We divided into twos, climbed the ravines, separated at the top, and were able to effectively cover four different areas of the mountain. I positioned myself under a small pine tree, near an outcrop of rocks, and waited, hoping to catch the elk coming down to feed. My rangefinder registered just over 500 yards to the timbers, a bit longer than I was comfortable shooting.

After about an hour, I looked up, and out of the timber came five elk. With the naked eye, I was pretty sure that four of them were cows, and one was a bull. The one I assumed to be a bull was larger in size and lighter in color. But all this was speculation. I could not see antlers at that distance, and it is illegal to shoot a spike bull. The bull had to have at least one 4-inch brow tine. Thank God for good glass!

My binoculars told me all I needed to know. Four cows could be clearly seen, and the bull was a shooter. I now knew exactly what my next course of action was to be.

In life, "good glass" is essential. We all face situations that leave us unsure what to do. Our human discernment and wisdom is limited. The great thing about being a Christian is that you have the Lord to help guide you each day. When you are unsure what to do and the future is unclear, it is amazing how time spent in prayer brings life into focus.

If you are trying to live your life without God's help, you are hunting without good glass. I often ask people two simple questions,

"If you put God into something, is it going to be better or worse?"

"If you take God out of something, is it going to be better or worse?'

Simple enough...

Chapter 16

IF YOU HAVE THE SHOT, TAKE IT!

"Be always sure you are right — then go ahead!" Davy Crockett

I glassed the bull, and determined it was a shooter. I then used my range finder. By then, the bull was standing 416 yards up the mountain from me. I immediately began to set up for the shot. I was seated under a small pine tree, so I reached over for my shooting sticks and rifle — a Remington 700, chambered for a .300 Winchester Mag cartridge. The 6.6x20 power Burris scope brought the elk into good focus, and I settled in for the shot.

I had practiced this shot. I knew that I could confidently shoot and hit my target up to 450 yards. The conditions were good, little to no wind, and I still had 25 minutes of legal shooting light.

One of the things I have learned as a hunter is this: if you have the shot, take it! You have to have the confidence to "pull the trigger" and you have to believe that you can make the shot. You cannot let fear or doubt control you.

The first *Pope and Young* Whitetail buck that I ever took with my bow, I watched for 40 minutes. There was a hot doe hovering under my tree stand, and she was attracting a lot of attention. There were three other bucks milling around beneath me, but the dominant buck was the one I wanted. He was hung up at 60 yards, giving me no shot. I was confident that I could make up to a 40 yard shot, and was hoping he would advance to a shooting lane I had opened up. I made up my mind that if he advanced down the trail and gave me a 40 yard shot, I would take it. Finally, he slowly walked towards the doe, and stopped where I had hoped he would. I came to full draw, settled in and released the arrow. It was a good shot, and a couple of hours later, I was standing over a 150 class Whitetail.

You can always talk yourself into waiting for a better shot, but if you can make the shot, and it is there, take it.

The bull elk was standing broadside up the mountain at 416 yards. I pulled the trigger, and the .300 Winchester Magnum roared. Yep, I pulled the trigger — didn't squeeze it. Knew it immediately. The four cow elk that were in front of the bull bolted forward about 100 yards. I am looking for the bull through my scope, trying to decide if I had hit him or not.

If your shooting mechanics are not perfect at that range, you are not going to hit your target. Most of us know in our gut if we made a good shot or not. A perfectly executed shot feels right. I didn't have that feeling.

I was fortunate, because the bull elk had followed the cows forward along the mountain. My scope found him 50 yards ahead of where he was when I had made my first shot. He was framed between two small pine trees, standing broadside, staring down the mountain towards me.

I chambered in a second round, settled in, and said to myself, "Ok, this time, do it right."

THANK GOD
FOR SECOND CHANCES

*"My first plan of escape having failed,
I now determined upon another." Buffalo Bill Cody*

You don't always get a second chance in this world. But I can tell you this, the God of the Bible is a God of second chances. One of the greatest attributes of God is His mercy and He showed me a little on that cold, November day.

I settled in for my second shot. First, I controlled my breathing, relaxed my body, and reacquired my target. I then slowly squeezed the trigger. The best shot you will ever make is one where the gun surprises you when it goes off. Pulling the trigger instead of squeezing it will always cause you to shoot to your right (for right-handers). At 416 yards, a slight pull to the right can cause you to miss by several yards. This time the shot felt right.

A Marine who attends my church told me that in Basic Training they teach the acronym, BRASS.

B — Breathe
R — Relax
A — Aim
S — Squeeze
S — Shoot

Like I said, the shot should be a surprise. When it is, you will almost always hit the bulls-eye.

As soon as I shot, I tried to reacquire the bull in my

scope to see if he was down. I couldn't find him, but the slope was covered in thick sagebrush, so he could be down. I glassed over to my left and watched the four cows bolting out of sight around the mountain. The bull was not behind them. I looked at my watch and saw that I only had about 20 minutes left of shooting light and a long hike up the mountain. The Montana preacher was hunting a quarter mile to my right, and he radioed to see if I had got one. I waited where I was till he came to me, then we started our climb up the mountain. It was a steep climb, and it took us some time to get to where the elk had been. It was completely dark by the time we arrived, and my bearings were a little off. The next hour we searched with flashlights, but failed to find the bull. Derek showed up to help and for another half hour, we searched.

Nothing.

If you have hunted much, you know what I was feeling. Nothing makes you as sick as the possibility that you missed or worse yet, wounded an animal. There was also the chance that in the dark, on a sagebrush-covered mountain slope, we might have just overlooked him.

We headed down towards the camp, and the Montana preacher asked, "What do you want to do in the morning?"

I immediately replied, "I have no choice. I might have missed, but I have to make sure. You three can hunt in the morning. I will wait till first light, then climb back up here and make a thorough search. I have to make sure."

He smiled. That's the answer he wanted to hear.

Chapter 18

HUNTING ETHICS

"Laws control the lesser man. Right conduct the greater one."
Mark Twain

There are three questions that should guide all of your actions while hunting: Is it legal? Is it safe? Is it ethical?

Every hunter is responsible to read and understand the hunting laws governing the state and region of your hunt. Proper laws are to be followed and respected. Is it legal?

Never put yourself or any other person at risk. Handle your firearm safely. Never point it at anything you do not intend to shoot. Be aware of what is beyond your target, and if you are in doubt, don't shoot. Is it safe?

Last of all, always ask yourself, is it ethical? Ethics is a code of conduct that goes beyond the law. Ethical behavior compels you to always show respect to others and to the game you are pursuing. Your ethics are a reflection of your own character. In short, ethics is doing the right thing.

My ethics dictated my decision to take Tuesday morning and thoroughly search for the bull elk that I shot at Monday evening. Any hunter who shoots at an animal, and then does not exercise due diligence to ensure that the animal is recovered and properly used is unethical.

The next morning, the Montana preacher and I climbed back up the mountain. He hunted for the first hour of light. I did not want to mess up his morning hunt, so I sat tight until he radioed me, then we met to search for the bull.

Within minutes, we found my elk. I cannot express how thankful I was! It was a fine young 5x5 bull, and I was blessed to harvest it.

It would have been easy to talk myself into believing that I had missed the bull. It would have been easier not to look for the bull than to look. But in hunting and in life, you do not do the easy thing, you do the right thing.

Here is a list of hunting ethics. These are the unwritten rules of conduct and consideration.

Always exercise fair chase when hunting animals. You do not give yourself an unfair or illegal advantage.

Know your firearm, and its limitations. Do not take shots beyond the range of your expertise.

Be 100% sure of what you are shooting at. Properly identify your game, make sure it is legal to shoot, and consider what is beyond your target. Never shoot in the direction of any building or any person.

Respect landowner's rights. Always secure permission before hunting on private property. When given permission, treat the privilege sacredly. Remember, you are a guest.

Respect other hunters. This is especially true while hunting on public land. You will share this land with other hunters, so be courteous and considerate of their hunt. If a hunter is hunting an area you intended to hunt, find another area. Don't purposely infringe upon his hunt.

This is not an exhaustive list. Ethics and etiquette are important in all areas of life. When in doubt as to what is appropriate behavior, consider this rule:

"Do unto others as you would want others to do unto you." That is still the gold standard of conduct.

Chapter 19

GENUINELY ENJOY
THE SUCCESS OF OTHERS

"The vice of envy is a confession of inferiority." Theodore Roosevelt

Elk hunting is in many ways a team sport. If you take an elk in the mountains, you will be glad that you are not hunting alone. If one in your group kills an elk, everyone pitches in to help get that elk off the mountain. When that's finished, you go back to hunting.

The Montana preacher who helped me find my elk enjoyed my success almost as much as I did. He congratulated me, then, together, we paused to thank the Good Lord for allowing us this experience. Here was an experienced elk hunter taking joy in the success of a rookie elk hunter. That meant a lot to me.

I have been on both sides of this. I have hunted Whitetail bucks for over 30 years. A successful hunter gets to a point where he takes as much pleasure out of helping a young man get his first deer as he would in killing a trophy himself.

Doug and Derek soon joined us. Again, there was genuine joy in sharing the experience with me. For the rest of the week, I was rooting for all of them to fill their tags and did everything I could to help make their hunts successful. On the last evening of the week-long hunt, the Montana preacher harvested a fine cow elk, and again we bowed together over it and thanked the Lord for His help.

One of the great keys to happiness is in learning to genuinely enjoy the success of others. Too many times, jealousy or envy ruins for everyone what should be a time of celebration. Take the time to congratulate people when they succeed. Shake their hand, slap them on the back, and tell them they did good! These moments don't come often enough in life, and should be enjoyed by all.

A good camera ought to be standard on every hunt. It is great to capture that moment. The picture will help you re-live that moment again and again in the future.

This fall, I had the opportunity to take my son-in-law, AJ, deer hunting. We had two days to hunt, and he had never killed a Whitetail buck. On the first evening, he took a basket rack 7 pointer — made a great shot on a running deer. You never saw a happier guy! Remember your first buck? I don't care what size it was, it was a trophy to you. I was pleased to share that moment with him, and I did everything I could to make that moment special for him.

As Doug and I drove home from Montana, I sent a text to Eric with a picture of my elk. He was thrilled for me, and asked if Doug had gotten one. I told him he didn't, and Eric sent back some encouragement.

"Tell him God makes elk everyday. He just isn't done putting all the antlers on Doug's yet." I thought that was a classy thing to say and I know it meant a lot to Doug.

If you can only be happy when you succeed, then your moments of happiness will be few and far between. But if you are genuinely happy for the success of others, then you can enjoy happiness much more often in life. Especially if you helped contribute in some small way to their success.

So learn this southern Indiana phrase: "Atta' boy!"

Chapter 20

YOU CAN CARRY MORE THAN YOU THINK

"When you stop fighting — that's death!" John Wayne

Once you down your elk, the work really begins. We removed the hide, then deboned the meat. The head, antlers, hide and about 225 pounds of meat were packed off the mountain. Thank God for good help.

I strapped the elk's head and antlers to my backpack and started down. It was heavier than I thought it would be. After a couple hundreds yards down the mountain, I began to question whether or not I was going to be able to carry it all the way to our camp.

Most of us can carry more than we think for longer than we think. I whispered a prayer, "Lord, I need some extra strength for this one."

Having been in the gospel ministry for over 30 years, it's not the first time I have had to pray that prayer. Everyone carries something. A pastor has his own burdens like anyone else. Then he also chooses to carry a lot of other people's burdens. I'm not complaining, not bragging, just telling the truth. So praying for extra strength isn't unusual.

If you don't have to ask God for strength on a regular basis, you aren't carrying enough.

I didn't know if I could make it down the mountain carrying all that weight, but I remembered something Doug had told me on the trip out. When he was in the Air Force, they lived by a "20x" rule. No matter how tired you were, when you didn't think you could run another step, you could always do 20 more. So that's what I did. Twenty steps, then twenty more. By the way, in real life, that is sometimes how you get through a day.

A strange thing happened. The more I walked the stronger I felt. Don't get me wrong, it wasn't easy. But prayer, perseverance and God's strength got me down that mountain.

You get to know someone when you spend a week hunting with him. Ron has pastored in Montana for over 27 years. He told me that God called him to his town because God knew he wouldn't quit. During their lives, he and his wife have experienced extreme heartache including financial reversals, ministry setbacks, losing their house to a fire, and the toughest — the death of their son. The details of these stories are not mine to tell, but some things they have gone through would have broken lesser Christians.

Whatever you are facing in life, you can make it! Complaining about how hard life is, or how heavy your burdens are doesn't get you off the mountain.

How did Ron and his wife make it? How do any of us make it when asked to carry more than we humanly can?

First, eliminate these two words from your vocabulary, "I can't." Then memorize this Bible verse because before this life is over you will need it more than once.

Philippians 4:13, "I can do all things through Christ which strengtheneth me."

On tough days, quote that verse and ask God for some extra strength. Then take 20 more steps, rest if you have to, but don't quit.

Persevere! With God's help, you'll make it.

Chapter 21

STOP AND ENJOY THE VIEW

"Here is your country. Cherish these natural wonders, cherish the natural resources, cherish the history… as a sacred heritage, for your children and your children's children." Theodore Roosevelt

During the week, I had several "Wow, I'm really here!" moments. I want to thank the Lord again for working everything out so that I could go on this hunt.

I am proud to be an American. I love this country. The song writer nailed it when he wrote *America the Beautiful*, because she is. I have been blessed to see much of it. Let me recommend some places to go and see as time and life allow (in no particular order).

1. View the red rock country of Sedona, Arizona. Then drive an hour north and see the grandest of canyons.

2. Spend a couple of days exploring Yellowstone's eerie, unearthly, breathtaking park. Then an extra day driving south to see the Grand Teton Mountains.

3. Experience a sunrise on the coast of South Carolina.

4. Watch the sun sink into the Pacific somewhere along northern California's rocky, redwood tree-lined coast.

5. Drive Tennessee's Smoky Mountains in the Fall.

6. Spend a weekend in South Dakota's surprising and stunning southwest corner. Then head east into the Badlands.

7. Start at Rocky Mountain National Park and drive south along Colorado's Peak-to-Peak Highway. Don't stop till you get to Golden.

8. Enjoy the Atlantic at an ocean-side sea food place in Rhode Island. Be sure to order a bowl of clam chowder.

9. Take a Memorial Day and tour the memorials in Washington D.C. While you are there, shake the hand of every veteran you see and tell them, "Thank you for your service." Then end the day watching the changing of the guard at Arlington National Cemetery.

10. Elk hunt the mountains of Montana.

There are still some places I would like to get to — not quite done with my bucket list yet. It's enjoyable to occasionally get away, but the best part of any trip I have ever taken is coming home. Jasonville, Indiana isn't on anyone's "must see" list, but to me, there is no place better on earth.

Learn to stop and enjoy the view where you live. My wife and I often take a walk down the gravel road in front of our house, and a thousand times in the past twenty years, I have looked at our small mini-farm and thanked God for lending me a piece of His earth. The "wow" moments in my life consist of sitting down to share a meal with friends, spending an afternoon with my grandchildren, or a quiet evening sitting with my wife on the porch — her reading and me writing — just enjoying being together. I've learned to cherish Sunday mornings at my church, weekday work projects and friendly banter at the local small town gathering places. I'm as happy fishing at an Indiana pond as I would be at a Smoky Mountain stream.

If you cannot learn to appreciate the everyday moments, then you will probably struggle to appreciate much of anything else in life. Every once in while, just stop what you're doing and look around.

And enjoy the view.

Chapter 22

WHEN YOU'VE CLIMBED YOUR LAST MOUNTAIN

"If you only know one thing for sure, know you're saved."
Robert Ross

I've made preparations for one last trip. It's all paid for and it didn't cost me a dime. And it promises to be the greatest trip of my life.

I know that if I died today, I would go to Heaven. That may sound prideful, but I assure you it's not. It is not because I am anything special, or because I am better than anyone else. Going to Heaven has nothing to do with what I am, but everything to do with what Jesus did for me.

Ephesians 2:8-9, For by grace are ye saved through faith; and that not of yourselves: it is the gift of God: Not of works, lest any man should boast.

If you have never received Jesus Christ as your Savior, I hope you will do so today. Consider carefully what the Bible explains to us concerning salvation.

1. Everyone of us has committed sins.

Romans 3:23, For all have sinned, and come short of the glory of God;

1 John 1:8, If we say that we have no sin, we deceive ourselves, and the truth is not in us.

The first step to getting saved is figuring out that you are lost. Our sins have separated us from God. They are what will keep us from Heaven. To be saved, a person must become convicted of his sins. When we understand our sinful state, and feel genuine sorrow for what we have done, then we have taken our first step towards salvation.

2. There is an eternal penalty for our sins.

Romans 5:12, Wherefore, as by one man sin entered into the world, and death by sin; and so death passed upon all men, for that all have sinned:

The punishment we deserve for our sins against God is an earthly, physical death and, afterwards, eternal dying in a place called hell.

Luke 16:22-24, And it came to pass, that the beggar died, and was carried by the angels into Abraham's bosom: the rich man also died, and was buried; And in hell he lift up his eyes, being in torments, and seeth Abraham afar off, and Lazarus in his bosom. And he cried and said, Father Abraham, have mercy on me, and send Lazarus, that he may dip the tip of his finger in water, and cool my tongue; for I am tormented in this flame.

3. Jesus died on the cross to pay for our sins.

In order to save mankind from hell, Jesus, God's only Son, came down to earth and lived a perfect life. He died on an old rugged cross — not for His sins, for He had none — but for the sins of the whole world. Jesus paid for your sins.

Romans 6:23, For the wages of sin is death; but the gift of God is eternal life through Jesus Christ our Lord.

1 Peter 2:21-25, For even hereunto were ye called: because Christ also suffered for us... Who his own self bare our sins in his own body on the tree, that we, being dead to sins, should live unto righteousness: by whose stripes ye were healed...

4. Every man chooses to accept Christ's payment, or to

insist on paying for his own sins.

God made us all with a free will. That means we can choose to be saved, or reject what God has done for us. I hope today you will choose to accept the salvation God, at great cost to Himself, so generously provided for you.

John 3:16-18, For God so loved the world, that he gave his only begotten Son, that whosoever believeth in him should not perish, but have everlasting life…. He that believeth on him is not condemned: but he that believeth not is condemned already, because he hath not believed in the name of the only begotten Son of God.

5. You can call upon Christ and be saved today.

Romans 10:9, That if thou shalt confess with thy mouth the Lord Jesus, and shalt believe in thine heart that God hath raised him from the dead, thou shalt be saved.

Romans 10:13, For whosoever shall call upon the name of the Lord shall be saved.

If you choose today to place your faith in Christ and what He did on the cross for you, and you are willing to pray to Him and ask for eternal life, you can be saved today.

Dear Jesus, I am sorry for the sins that I have committed against you. Thank you for sending your Son, Jesus Christ, to pay for my sins. I do believe in His death, burial and resurrection and understand that Jesus did all this for me. I want to be saved today, and become a child of God. Thank you for saving me. Amen.

I hope you have trusted Christ today as your Savior. If so, go to my website and let me know about your decision. I will be glad to send you some free materials that will help you grow in your newly found faith.

May God bless you as you climb your next mountain.

About the Author

Jerry Ross is the senior pastor of the Blessed Hope Baptist Church of Jasonville, Indiana. In addition, he is an author, conference speaker, and avid outdoorsman.

Other Titles by the Author

The Teenage Years of Jesus Christ
The Childhood Years of Jesus Christ
Stay in the Castle
The Seven Royal Laws of Courtship
Is Your Youth Group Dead or Alive?
Grace Will Lead Me Home
21 Tenets of Biblical Masculinity
21 Tenets of Biblical Femininity (Jerry & Sheryl Ross)
104 Teen Training Hour Lessons
Mountain Lessons

Ultimate Goal Publications
Jasonville, Indiana
www.stayinthecastle.com
(812) 665-4375